Reverberation

Matthew López is the author of *The Inheritance*, which premiered in 2018 at the Young Vic before transferring to the West End and Broadway. Matthew won the Tony, Olivier, *Evening Standard*, Drama Desk, London Critics Circle, Outer Critics Circle, Drama League, and GLAAD Awards for Best Play for *The Inheritance*. His play *The Sentinels* premiered in London in 2011 as part of Headlong Theatre's *Decade* plays. Other plays include *The Whipping Man, Somewhere, The Legend of Georgia McBride*, and *Zoey's Perfect Wedding*. In 2023, Matthew co-wrote and directed the film adaptation of *Red, White and Royal Blue*.

by the same author

THE INHERITANCE

MATTHEW LÓPEZ

Reverberation

faber

First published in 2024
by Faber and Faber Limited
The Bindery, 51 Hatton Garden, London EC1N 8HN
Typeset by Agnesi Text, Hadleigh, Suffolk
Printed in England by CPI Group (UK) Ltd, Croydon CR0 4YY

All rights reserved

© Matthew López, 2024

Matthew López is hereby identified as author
of this work in accordance with Section 77 of the
Copyright, Designs and Patents Act 1988

All rights whatsoever in this work, amateur or professional,
are strictly reserved. Applications for permission for any use
whatsoever including performance rights must be made in
advance, prior to any such proposed use, to Creative Artists Agency
(attn: Kevin Lin), 405 Lexington Avenue, 19th Floor,
New York, NY 10174, USA

No performance may be given unless a licence
has first been obtained

This book is sold subject to the condition that it shall not,
by way of trade or otherwise, be lent, resold, hired out
or otherwise circulated without the publisher's prior consent
in any form of binding or cover other than that in which
it is published and without a similar condition including
this condition being imposed on the subsequent purchaser

A CIP record for this book is available from the British Library

ISBN 978–0–571–39478–4

Printed and bound in the UK on FSC® certified paper in line with our continuing
commitment to ethical business practices, sustainability and the environment.
For further information see faber.co.uk/environmental-policy

9780571394784

1 2 4 6 8 10 9 7 5 3

Characters

Jonathan

Claire

Wes

Reverberation was first performed at Hartford Stage, Hartford, Connecticut, on 19 February 2015.

The cast was as follows:

Jonathan Luke Macfarlane
Claire Aya Cash
Wes Carl Lundstedt

Director Maxwell Williams
Set Design Andromache Chalfant
Costume Design Linda Cho
Lighting Design Matthew Richards
Sound Design Tei Blow
Dramaturg Elizabeth Williamson
Stage Manager Marisa Levy
Fight Director J. Allen Suddeth
Production Manager Bryan T. Holcombe
Assistant Stage Manager Arielle Goldstein
Assistant Director Sarah Hartmann
Production Assistant Chandalae Nyswonger

The European premiere of *Reverberation* was given at Bristol Old Vic, in association with Glass Half Full Productions, on 2 October 2024. The cast was as follows:

Claire Eleanor Tomlinson
Jonathan Michael Ahomka-Lindsay
Wes Jack Gibson

Director Jack Sain
Set and Costume Designer Ti Green
Lighting Designer Robbie Butler
Video Designer Daniel Denton
Sound Designer and Composer Nicola T. Chang
Intimacy Coordinator Robbie Taylor Hunt
Movement Director Jade Hackett
Casting Director Matilda James CDG
Dialect Coach Aundrea Fudge
Voice Coach Carol Fairlamb
Assistant Director (supported by Bath Spa University) Lex Kaby
Costume Supervisor Anna Dixon
Linbury Design Associate Peiyao Wang
Dramatherapist Samantha Adams

Company Stage Manager Lucy Topham
Deputy Stage Manager Verity Clayton
Assistant Stage Manager Eve Richardson

FOR BRISTOL OLD VIC

Artistic Director Nancy Medina
Executive Director Charlotte Geeves
Director of Producing and Programming Jessica Campbell
Producer Ruby Gilmour
Assistant Producer Charlotte Churm
Literary Manager Ben Atterbury
Productions and Operations Director David Harraway
Production Manager Aled Thomas

FOR GLASS HALF FULL PRODUCTIONS

UK Producer Leila Sykes
Founder & Producer Gareth Lake

REVERBERATION

For Elizabeth Williamson

Act One

1 AFTER WORK

Two apartments in Tottenham, North London: one upstairs from the other and both identically constructed. The upstairs apartment is sparsely furnished. Nothing more than an air mattress in the bedroom and a cheap collapsible clothing rack. Women's clothes are strewn about – from bras and panties to expensive dresses. Nothing is treated with care. The living room is equally spartan: a camping chair in front of a small, 1990s television that rests on the floor. The walls are bare. Take-out containers and empty wine bottles litter the kitchen countertop.

The downstairs apartment, by contrast, is packed with possessions. Photographs and knick-knacks everywhere. Shelves groan under the weight of hundreds of books. A decent stereo system. A work table that overflows with personal papers, unopened mail, and half-read books and magazines. Large canvases of original paintings cover the walls.

Upstairs suggests transience. Downstairs suggests permanence.

At rise, both apartments are dark. Gradually we notice that from the downstairs bedroom we can hear the sound of two men having sex. Their noise and intensity rises with the lights as we reveal Jonathan (thirty) fucking Wes (twenty-one). It's pretty intense. Jonathan devours Wes, constantly feeling his body, kissing him. Wes is overwhelmed by Jonathan's passionate attentions. Wes is a noisy lay, responding vocally to every thrust, his body reacting instantly to every touch from Jonathan, every kiss and caress. Jonathan, on the other hand, is nearly silent. He is solely focused on Wes's body, on his lips and neck. They fuck for a while. Long enough for us to feel like voyeurs.

The fucking grows in intensity. Jonathan works his way up to his orgasm. Wes encourages him along. Eventually, Jonathan comes. He then completely collapses into Wes's arms. They hold each other in for a few moments. Everything settles into a serene silence.

Then Wes whispers into Jonathan's ear, kisses him, gets up and heads naked to the bathroom.

Jonathan sits up and stares blankly for a moment. He then gets up and heads naked to the living room. Both Jonathan's and Wes's clothes are strewn about on the floor and sofa, exactly where they left them when they tore them off each other. Jonathan grabs one of the two glasses of booze that sit on his coffee table – their unfinished pre-sex cocktails – and downs it. He pours another and drinks it quickly.

The toilet flushes. Jonathan grabs his clothes off the floor and starts to dress. Wes emerges from the bathroom, still naked.

Wes Christ, I'm knackered. That was – (*Sees Jonathan isn't there.*) Hey, where'd you go?

Wes comes in from the bedroom.

You're getting dressed?

Jonathan I thought we were done.

Wes *You* might be.

Jonathan It's pretty late / and I have a big day tomorrow.

Wes It's only / eleven thirty.

Jonathan I gotta be up pretty early.

Pause.

Wes That was . . . I think that was, like, the greatest sex I've ever had, ever.
 Wasn't it?
 You just . . . devoured me. At one point I thought you were actually going to eat me.

Jonathan Listen / I really should –

Wes Could I have some water?

Jonathan Sure.

Jonathan pours Wes a glass of water.

Wes You look different from your pictures. Less, um, less boyish.

Jonathan Are you calling me old?

Wes I'm calling your pictures old. I mean, I knew you were fit but I wasn't expecting those muscles when you opened the door. I thought you were the bouncer.

Jonathan Oh. Yeah. I've started working out.

Wes Yeah, I can tell.
Pretty mental that we live so close, huh? I never see you out and about.

Jonathan I don't go out a lot.

Wes How old are you?

Jonathan Thirty.

Wes Wow. You're like the oldest guy I've ever had sex with.

Jonathan Thank you?

Wes No, thank you.

Jonathan You're . . . ?

Wes Twenty-one.

Jonathan Right.

Wes I think we're pretty good at this, you and me. Good chemistry.

Jonathan Yeah.

Wes Maybe we should make this a regular thing.

Jonathan It's probably better if we just left this a one-time thing.

Wes Are you kidding? I live two hundred metres away!

Jonathan I just . . . I'm not really looking for that.

Wes You know your phone doesn't come with Grindr pre-installed.

Wes puts his arms around Jonathan's neck and gives him the hard stare. Jonathan is not immune to Wes's allure. He puts his hands on Wes's hips and pulls him closer. Wes leans in for a kiss. But then:

Jonathan I have to work in the morning.

Wes You're killing me.

Jonathan I'm sorry. It's late and I –

Wes Yeah. Okay. Yeah, it's cool.

Wes pulls away and starts hunting for his clothes.

I can always go back on Grindr, right?

Jonathan Or read a book.

Wes Or write a symphony. There's a million things I could be doing right now.

Wes dresses. Annoyed, awkward silence as he does.

Jonathan I, ah . . .

Wes Yeah?

Jonathan I didn't mean 'read a book' as if you didn't ever.

Wes I know.

Jonathan I didn't mean to insinuate that you don't read because you're –

Wes A bottom?

Jonathan No, I meant –

Wes I know what you meant.

Wes looks at Jonathan's books.

You own a lot of books.

Jonathan Yeah.

Wes Well, of course you do. You're a top.
You haven't actually read all of these, have you?

Jonathan Maybe half?

Wes I chucked most of my books when I moved here.

Jonathan Why?

Wes They were heavy.

Jonathan But they're your books.

Wes That's what Kindles are for.

Jonathan That's just not the same.

Wes Why? Same words.

Jonathan A book is more than just the words on the page.

Wes You have to admit that they're helpful.

Jonathan It's the width of the margins, the smell, the paper stock. It's tactile, you know.

Wes feels Jonathan's arms.

Wes *You're* tactile.

Jonathan Reading is a physical act.

Wes Like fucking.

Wes starts rubbing Jonathan's arms and chest.

Jonathan You don't just engage with the ideas in the book, you engage with the book itself. Its size, its dimensions. Is it a hardcover or paperback?

Wes Hard, definitely hard.

Wes's hands move to Jonathan's arse.

Jonathan But on a Kindle, every book has only one edition and it's the same as every other book. It obliterates uniqueness.

Wes You know how to catch a unique animal? Unique up on it.

Jonathan takes Wes's hands in his and uses them to illustrate his point:

Jonathan On a Kindle, *The Happy Prince* weighs exactly the same as *War and Peace*. But that's not the case when you read the books. With the books, you feel the weight of the Tolstoy in your hands – like the whole of Russian history living inside those thousands of pages. Or, with the Wilde, the weightlessness of a world so precious, it might float away if you were to let it go. As if you were reading a feather.

Their fingers intertwine. Wes kisses Jonathan's fingers one by one.

A book is typeset. Actual thought goes into what font to use and how it's laid out. Garamond. Cambria. Baskerville. If that wasn't important, they wouldn't bother to put that note at the end of so many books. Kindles just reduce all that to Times New Roman. And if everything is read in the same font, if everything looks the same, if it weighs the same, smells the same, feels the same . . . it starts to become the same. And then nothing is special.

Wes puts his hands up inside Jonathan's shirt. Jonathan allows him to do this, wrapping his arms around Wes. Their faces are so close to each other now.

And don't get me started on the art of book covers, the civic necessity of libraries and the unalloyed joys of browsing through bookshops, particularly, if possible, on a rainy afternoon after you've just seen a film.

They kiss deeply. It lasts a while. Then they pull away and Wes just stares at him, falling hopelessly in love.

Wes You know how to catch a tame animal?

Jonathan How?

Wes Tame way.

They kiss. Then:

What's your favourite book?

Jonathan Don't ask me that.

Wes You don't have a favourite?

Jonathan I have too many favourites.

Wes Pick one.

Jonathan looks at the shelf, thinks a moment, then pulls one down, hands it to Wes.

Another Country by James Baldwin.

Jonathan Yeah, it's –

Wes What do you love about it?

Jonathan Everything. The world, the ideas, the characters, the feeling.

Wes Kinda like the 'itness' of it?

Jonathan Yeah. Kinda. You've not – ?

Wes Haven't gotten to it yet.

Jonathan I must have read it four, maybe five times.

Wes Wow. Why?

Jonathan I like . . . going back into the world. Kinda like visiting with an old friend.

Wes With the characters, you mean?

Jonathan Yeah, but more like with Baldwin himself. It's . . . I dunno . . . like I have a relationship with him. Like he gets me. That doesn't make sense, but –

Wes It does.

Pause.

Jonathan You can, um, you can take it, if you want.

Wes You're going to give your favourite book to a total stranger?

Jonathan It's not like it's a first edition or anything.

Wes Oh man, it would have been so much cooler if you'd said, 'You're not a stranger any more.'

Jonathan Take it. You'll love it.

Wes What I'd really love to is to read it and then return it to you.

Jonathan You don't . . . have to do that.

Wes But I'd like to.

Silence. A fairly long, uncertain one.

I once heard that we don't pick the books, the books pick us. Do you believe that?

Jonathan I don't know.

Wes I guess we'll find out.

Silence.

I should probably get out of your hair, huh?

Jonathan Oh. Yeah. Okay.

Wes I mean, I can stay if you want.

Pause.

Jonathan No, I should get to bed.

Wes I could stay over.

Jonathan I don't sleep very well when someone else is –

Wes Yeah, me either.

Jonathan Yeah.

Wes So let's not sleep, then.

Wes pulls him into a kiss. Jonathan resists at first but Wes is one hell of a good kisser and this one is deep, wet and seductive. Then:

Jonathan I really need to get to bed.

Wes is disappointed but tries not to show it.

Wes Okay. Yeah. See you around.

Jonathan walks Wes to the door, opens it. They stand there. They kiss again.

Jonathan What's your name?

Wes I'm Wes.

Jonathan I'm Jonathan.

Wes Nice to meet you, Jonathan.

Jonathan Yes. Well. Good night.

Wes Good night.

Wes leaves. Jonathan closes the door. Wes looks down at the book in his hands, then over at the closed door. He sighs. Then he heads down the stairs into the lobby and out the front door.

Jonathan pours another drink and sits down on the sofa.

Upstairs, the sound of someone walking across the floor. The apartment is too dark to see anyone.

2 BEFORE WORK

Downstairs, Jonathan is making breakfast. Briefly about his appearance: he's solidly built with a toned/muscled gym body. He's a simple jeans, T-shirt and hoodie kind of a guy. Everything about his appearance suggests someone who'd prefer not to be noticed.

Upstairs, Claire (twenty-nine, American) is getting ready for work. She is wearing something very stylish. She is a very stylish girl. She clip-clops across the floor in her high-heeled shoes.

Jonathan hears her upstairs and is stopped in his tracks by the sound. While she scurries around the apartment to get ready to leave, he stares up at his ceiling, as if transfixed by the noise. He unconsciously begins to follow her around her apartment by following her sounds. Eventually they lead him to his apartment door, which fills him with sudden fear.

While Claire stops to check herself out one last time in a mirror she keeps by the door, Jonathan wills himself to open the door. He seems incapable of it.

Hands trembling, he forces himself to quickly unlock the door and open it. He stands there with the door open, staring out into the hall.

Suddenly, Claire leaves her apartment and comes bounding down the stairs, catching him before he can go back inside.

Claire Oh my God, hi! Do you live on this floor?

Pause.

Jonathan Uh . . .

Claire I just moved in upstairs. You seem pretty all right.

Jonathan That's a matter of perspective, I suppose.

Claire I was afraid it would just be hipsters and soccer fans living out here but you . . . well. *Are* you a hipster?

Jonathan No.

Claire Okay, then. I'm Claire.

Pause.

I hope I'm not too loud or anything.

Jonathan What?

Claire Upstairs. My shoes, sometimes they . . . clip-clop, clip-clop, you know.

Jonathan I . . . I haven't noticed anything.

Claire Oh good! Well, that's a good start. I can be a little loud sometimes. Just don't be afraid to tell me. Are you leaving for work?

Jonathan Oh. Um . . .

Claire Are you headed out? Should we walk to the train together? I need to grab a coffee. And maybe a bagel. I'm starving! Do they even have bagels in London? Or is it all clotted cream and scones?

Pause.

Jonathan You know, I just remembered I left something in my bedroom that I –

Claire I don't mind waiting.

Jonathan The thing is I, ah, I don't remember where I put it.

Claire Maybe I can help you look for it.

Jonathan I'm good, thanks.

Jonathan heads back inside, closing his door on her.

Claire Okay, so I'll just see you around.

Claire dies a little, mouthing, 'Oh my God, Claire' to herself. They stand on either side of the door: him, waiting for her to leave; her, waiting for him to re-emerge.

Finally, she gives up and goes clip-clopping down the stairs and out the building. He sinks down to the floor, sitting against the door, waiting for it to be clear to leave.

3 AFTER WORK

A few nights later. Claire's apartment is dark. Jonathan sits, on his phone. A drink before him.

Claire enters the building, wearing a gorgeous dress. She gets to her apartment, and clip-clops inside. Jonathan hears, looks up, then a Grindr notification brings his attention back to his phone.

Claire moves to her bedroom and tries to unzip her dress. The zipper is stuck. She struggles, but it's no good. She goes to her living room and collapses onto the camping chair, grabs her remote and turns on the television.

Jonathan grabs his phone and dials a number.

Jonathan Hi, it's . . .
Yeah.
Cool.
Yeah, I do.
Yeah, sounds good.
Yeah. So . . .
Okay. Call me when you're close.
Bye.

He hangs up and pours a fresh drink. As he does, Claire tries the zipper again. Fails. She then comes out of her apartment, and goes down to his floor and knocks on his door.

Yes?

Claire Hey, it's Claire.

Pause.

Jonathan Who?

Claire Your neighbour. Upstairs?
 The clip-clop girl.
 I'm sorry to bother you but I'm having a bit of an emergency and I need some help.

Jonathan opens the door.

Hey, I'm so sorry to bother you but I'm stuck in this dress. You think you could unzip me?

Claire turns her back to him, revealing her zipper.

Jonathan Oh. Sure.

Claire Thanks.

He tries.

Jonathan It's stuck.

Claire Yeah. Can you – ?

He tries again. As he does, she takes a peek into his apartment.

Oooh, wow. You're really settled in here, aren't you?
 How stuck is it?

Jonathan It's, um, it's pretty snagged.

Claire Fuuuuuuuuck!

Jonathan Should I . . .?

Claire Tug it.
 He does. Nothing.

Harder.

He tugs even harder. Nothing.

Jonathan I can't . . . I can't get it.

Claire Fuck! My! Fucking! Life!

Jonathan Sorry. Look, I / really need to –

Claire I am so fucked!

Jonathan Look, I –

Claire Why does this shit always happen to me?

She tries to grab at the zipper in frustration. A bit of a dog chasing its tail.

Fuck me, goddamnit!

She collapses onto the sofa.

Could I please have a drink?

Jonathan Well, actually I –

Claire Whatever you're having. I don't care.

No response from Jonathan other than growing discomfort. They look at each other. She smiles. He pours a drink for her.

It's weird being down here. You know, because our apartments are exactly the same? It's like being given a glimpse of what my life would be like if I hadn't made every wrong decision in the book. You're such a grown-up. You own art and everything.

Jonathan Oh, you know.

Claire These pieces are so interesting. So bold and striking. But they're also . . . what – ?

Jonathan Kind. They're kind and compassionate.

Claire Who painted / them?

Jonathan That's a nice dress.

Claire 'Nice'? The paintings are kind and compassionate but my dress is 'nice'?

Jonathan That dress is a Hitchcock blonde.

Claire is delighted by that. She pulls the price tag out.

Claire And it costs a fortune. See?
Oh, go on. You know you want to.

He peeks at the price tag.

Jonathan What the fuck?

Claire Right?

Jonathan How can you afford that?

Claire I can't! Why do you think the tag's still on? I work at Liberty's. I borrowed it for the night.

Jonathan They let you do that?

Claire They don't know they let me do that. Which is why Cinderella has got to get this little number back to the store before anyone notices it's gone. If Cinderella can get the fucking thing off.

Jonathan is charmed. But then he realises . . .

Jonathan So you're kinda fucked, aren't you?

Claire Beyond fucked.

Jonathan Let me try again.

He looks at the zipper again, really examining it.

Okay, so . . .

Claire Give it to me, doc.

Jonathan You can see the lining sticking through. And it's all, like, chewed up by the zip. That's probably not good, is it?

Claire That . . . is a goddamned epic Chernobyl-like disaster. Fuck me!!! It was just going to be for tonight. I was going to get to work early and put it back and no one would have known.

Jonathan takes their glasses and returns to the kitchen to refill them.

I mean he took me to Annabel's tonight. What was I supposed to do? Go in last season? I'm so fucked.

Jonathan's phone rings.

Do you need to get that?

Jonathan Um . . . yeah, probably.

She looks down at the phone.

Claire 'Withheld Number', how mysterious. Is it your dealer?

Jonathan returns with the drink.

Jonathan No.

Claire Are you the dealer?

Jonathan No.

Claire Are you an escort?

Jonathan Tons of people get anonymous calls.

Claire Drug dealers and escorts.

The phone stops ringing.

Now we'll never know.

He hands over her drink. She hands over his phone.

What do you do for a living?

Jonathan Nothing exciting.

Claire Are you a lawyer?

Jonathan No.

Claire A writer?

Jonathan No.

Claire An actor? A teacher? A gymnast! I'll keep guessing until you tell me.

Jonathan I'm an illustrator.

Claire What, like Pixar movies?

Jonathan That's an animator. I do graphic novels sometimes. Um . . . sometimes children's books.

Claire goes weak.

Claire That is SO SWEET!

Jonathan And, uh . . . I do work for a friend who started his own greeting card company during lockdown.

Claire Are these your illustrations?

She bounds over to the table.

Jonathan Oh . . .

She starts rifling through his sketches.

Claire Look at these! You're so talented!

Jonathan They're just sketches.

Claire Are these for Valentine's Day?

Jonathan No, they're –

Claire What?

Jonathan They're sympathy cards. Condolences.

Claire Oh.
Show me your Valentine's cards.

Jonathan I'm not working on one right now.

Claire You, ah, you do a lot of these, um, sympathy things?

Jonathan I do all kinds. It's just . . . these are what I'm best at.

Claire Really? That's. Why?

Jonathan Oh, ah, you know. It's, ah. Because saying 'I'm sorry this happened to you' is not something that comes easily to most people. They just . . . don't know what to say. So I . . . help them.

Claire What's your name, cowboy?

Jonathan Oh, um, Jonathan.

Claire Hi, Jonathan.

Jonathan Hi . . .

Claire Claire.

Jonathan Hi, Claire.

Claire You're sweet, you know that?

Jonathan I'm not / sweet.

Claire You're just dripping honey out of every pore.

Jonathan I've said three words to you.

Claire All of them sweet.

Jonathan I'm not sweet.

Claire What, then?

A pause.

Jonathan Dangerous.

This is a surprising answer. She is doubly, triply intrigued. He instantly regrets saying that.

Claire Oooh! What makes you dangerous?

Jonathan Nothing. I'm not actually dangerous.

Claire Bullshit. You're definitely a little dangerous or else why would you have / said it?

Jonathan I don't know why I said it. It was the first word that / popped into my head.

Claire Because in some way it's true.

Jonathan No.

Claire Or you want it to be true. I bet you've got a little danger in you.

Jonathan You'd lose that bet.

Claire Maybe we should find out.

Jonathan Ah –

Claire See how far you can go.

Jonathan You might be disappointed.

Claire You wanna be a little bad?

Jonathan I –

Claire You wanna fuck me?

Silence.

Jonathan Listen . . .

The realisation that she's crossed a major line quickly sinks in.

Claire Oh, God, I'm so sorry. I thought that's where we were going.

Jonathan Um –

Claire Weren't we going there?

Jonathan I wasn't.

Claire Jesus, I'm sorry.

Jonathan No.

Claire Oh God, you were right. Sweet, not dangerous.

Jonathan I never said sweet. I still object to / sweet.

Claire I'm sorry, look, I've been drinking. And I'm an asshole. / A real . . . Jesus, Claire.

Jonathan No.

She heads for the door.

No, really –

Claire Thank you for your help. Thank you for the drink. Sorry I . . . you seem to be just a sw— / Okay, bye.

Jonathan There's nothing to be embarrassed about.

Claire scurries up the stairs and into her apartment, slamming the door behind her.
Jonathan's phone rings again. He hesitates, then answers.

Hey.
 Yeah, I'm sorry, I got . . . I was . . . just getting ready. I didn't hear the –
 Yes.
 Yes, I do.
 Okay. 27. Hit the buzzer next to '27'.
 Okay.

Jonathan hangs up, pours himself another drink.
Claire tugs on the zipper with all her might. It does not budge. She grows more desperate with every tug. A moment, then she opens a drawer and pulls out a pair of scissors. She puts them to the top of the dress nearest the zipper, takes a breath and then makes a big, awful cut down the side. Once the cut is large enough, she wiggles out of the dress, letting it fall to the floor. She then sits on her bed, clutching the ruined dress.
Jonathan's buzzer goes off. He goes to it and pushes a button.

Hey.

Male Voice on Intercom Hey, man.

Jonathan Up the stairs. Flat 27.

Male Voice on Buzzer Cool.

Jonathan buzzes the guy in. We hear the lobby door open and the guy walk in. We then hear the lobby door close and the guy climbing the stairs. As this is happening, Jonathan undresses.

4 LATER THAT NIGHT

Jonathan sits on his sofa, half dressed, clutching a drink, much like how we left him at the end of Scene 1. Except this time he is very drunk. Claire is asleep in her apartment.

Jonathan stands and notices that the front door is open. He stumbles over to close it. He instead looks out into the hallway and up at Claire's floor. He stares at it a moment, then wanders over to the stairs leading up. He puts his foot on the bottom step. He tries to will himself to climb the stairs but he can't. He waits and tries once again but he just can't bring himself to do it. He returns to his apartment, slamming the door behind him. At this, Claire wakes up and slowly sits up, listening to Jonathan below. He paces, growing agitated. He doesn't know what to do with himself. He then lets out an anguished cry. It is loud and deeply pained. He lets out another and another.

Jonathan then looks up at the large paintings on the wall. They bring him to silence. He stares at them a moment, then approaches one, placing his hands on it. Communing with it. The painting soothes him, quiets him.

Claire continues to sit up and stare down at the floor.

5 AFTER WORK

A few nights later. Claire is out. Jonathan is on the phone. An open bottle on the table, a drink in his hand.

Jonathan Look, Mum, I can't keep having this conversation with you. I'm not coming home for Christmas this year. End of story.

No, you don't need to put Dad on the line.

No, I don't want . . .

One, two, three.

Hi, Dad.

No, it isn't a question of money. I just don't feel like coming home this year.

Yes, I know it's been a while since I –

I just can't this year, okay? Please don't make me –

I don't know. Maybe I'll cook.

Oh my God, Mum. I burned the plantains once.

I'm fine, I promise.

A beat.

Hey, listen, guys, I need to run.

No, it's just that I have work to do and I –

No, I don't think I can do New Year, either.

A beat.

Okay, bye, Mum. I'll –

A beat.

No, Dad, nothing's wrong.

I'm holding up fine, I promise.

Yes, I would tell you.

Look, Dad, I know you mean well but I just don't wanna talk about it.

Because I don't.

Because I don't.

BECAUSE I DON'T!!!

I'm sorry.

I'm sorry, Dad.

No, I – Yeah.

Yeah, okay.

Yes, sir.

Yes, sir.

Uh-huh.

Right.

Yeah.

He hangs up, pours a drink. He goes to his laptop, opens it. A few clicks and then he grabs his phone and dials a number from off the screen.

   Claire comes home. She changes out of her work clothes.

Hey, it's . . .
   Yeah.
   Not much, man. Just saw your message.
   I don't know. You tell me.
   Cool.
   You wanna come here?
   Tottenham.
   It's not that far. Where are you?
   It's like half an hour from central.
   It's the same way in both directions. It's not like we have a wormhole that gets us to Soho in seconds.
   So why don't you come here?
   No, it's, ah, it's difficult for me to go into the city.
   No, I'm not 'crippled', I . . .
   I just . . . look, why don't you just come here?
   I'm not trying to be difficult, I just don't like going out after –
   Okay. Yeah, sorry to waste your time.

He hangs up. He pours another drink. He plucks a book from the shelf, turns on some music, grabs his phone and turns on Grindr. He moves to his sofa and reads, occasionally responding to a Grindr alert that tumbles in.

   Claire, meanwhile, has grabbed some food from the kitchen, sat down on her camping chair and turned on the television.

   We sit with them a moment, Jonathan's music and occasional Grindr alerts downstairs and Claire's television upstairs.

   A thunderclap. They both look up at their windows a moment, then return to their activities.

6 MONDAY MORNING

Claire's rushing to get to work on time while Jonathan makes himself breakfast. Once again he traces her traffic pattern but this time merely following her with his eyes from time to time. She eventually makes it out of the door and down the stairs. Jonathan goes over to open his door just as she's passing.

Jonathan Hey.

Claire Oh, hey.

Jonathan Busy weekend?

Claire Endless.

Jonathan Have any fun?

Claire I always have fun.

Jonathan What was his name?

Claire Phil. Ed? Phil.

Pause.

Jonathan What, ah, whatever happened with that dress?

Claire Oh God, I don't want to talk about it.

Jonathan Oh. Yeah. Okay.

Claire I had to cut it off!

Jonathan No! Did they make you pay for it?

Claire No.

Jonathan Oh. How / did you –

Claire I quit before they found out it was missing.

Jonathan Oh. So what / are you –

Claire I start at Selfridges today.

Jonathan Oh good.

Claire Yeah. The people are nicer there. Less stuck-up.

Jonathan Nice.

Claire Yeah.

  Silence a moment.

(*Starting to go.*) Well, anyway . . .

Jonathan Do you want to have dinner sometime this week?

Claire Oh. Sure. Just me?

Jonathan You can bring Phil if you want.

Claire God, no.

Jonathan Then just the two of us. Something low key. I can cook.

Claire Are you a good cook?

Jonathan I'm a great cook.

Claire I believe that.

Jonathan How's tonight?

Claire Tonight? Ah, tonight's no good. I have a date.

Jonathan Phil?

Claire Ed.

Jonathan Tuesday?

Claire I have to work. Wednesday?

Jonathan Wednesday's good.

Claire Boy, you really are popular, aren't you? Wednesday, then.

Jonathan Great. Is there anything you don't eat?

Claire The fork.

He smiles.

What are you doing today?

Jonathan Just working from home.

Claire Do you ever leave the house?

Jonathan Oh, um . . .

Claire (*sensing she's misstepped*) Forget I said anything. Erase it from your mind. Just remember me as I am right now: charming and late for work. See ya later, alligator.

She leaves and he stays there a moment, her words still in his mind. He wills himself to take a tentative step out into the hallway. This should take as long as it needs to. He might even land one foot outside but as soon as he does, or as soon as he's properly frightened, he abandons the project and rushes back inside, slamming the door behind him in fear. His breath is fast. He can feel the sweat pouring down his shirt. He stands in his now closed doorway looking at his apartment – his refuge, and his prison.

7 AFTER WORK

Jonathan and Claire sit at his table. Dinner is finished.

Claire And so I go downstairs. We're talking five in the morning. I mean, I'm always up for a party / but come on!

Jonathan I believe that.

Claire So I knock on his door. Pound, really. Furious. And he comes lumbering out, this big, fat, sweaty guy. And I say, 'It is five o'clock in the morning! Time for your party to be over!'

Jonathan Wow.

Claire But wait . . .

So he takes one giant, drunken step out into the hallway and he gets right in my face and says: 'If you bother me one more time about the music coming from my apartment, I will snap your neck like a turkey!' And then he goes back into his apartment and slams his door in my face.

So I go back up to my apartment. Now I'm quaking with rage and I take my stereo speaker and put it face down on the floor and I start to play Britney Spears at full blast.

Jonathan Right on.

Claire So we've got Death Metal downstairs and 'Hit Me Baby One More Time' upstairs. And I've still got *Oops! . . . I Did It Again*, *In the Zone*, and *Blackout* to get through so I've got all the time in the world, you know? So it's just a standoff.

Jonathan And who won?

Claire Well . . . the thing is I'd been stealing his wifi for months at this point and he must've known because he kicked me off and my Spotify crapped out.

Jonathan face-palms.

So the next day at work, I went onto Rightmove and found this place. And that's how I became your neighbour.

Jonathan People can be so frightening. I'm amazed you can tell that story so charmingly.

Claire What am I gonna do? Fall apart? Fuck him. He doesn't deserve that from me. 'Don't Go Knockin' On My Door', am I right?

Jonathan I don't get that reference.

Claire Oh, I see you're that kinda gay. How long have you been here?

Jonathan Almost ten years?

Claire You've been in this apartment for TEN YEARS?

Jonathan Almost ten. And actually, I was in your apartment at first. And then I, I moved down here last year.

Claire Why? Are there mice?

Jonathan No.

Claire You can tell me. I'm tough. The last story notwithstanding.

Jonathan There are no mice.

Claire A ghost?

Jonathan I don't believe in ghosts.

Claire So what, then?

Jonathan Nothing. I just wanted a change.

Claire Man, when I want a change, I need another continent.

Jonathan Where were you before you were here?

Claire Vegas, baby!

Jonathan Were you a showgirl?

Claire With these legs I could be. I'd gone there on vacation, met a guy, stayed. He was a dealer. Cards, not drugs. I was living in LA at the time and needed to get away from my boyfriend. He was a dealer, too. Drugs, not cards. Before that, San Francisco and then Boston before that.

Jonathan Wow, so –

Claire Paris for a year. That was cool. Atlanta for six months. That wasn't so cool. Denver, briefly. Miami for far too long. And, before that, home with Mom and Dad.

Jonathan Wow, that's . . . quite a life. How long do you think you'll be in London?

Claire I like it here. I think I'll stay forever.

Jonathan Why don't I believe you?

She smiles. He's clearly paying attention.

What makes you decide to leave a place when you do?

Claire I just know the time is right and I go, no looking back, no explanations.

Jonathan Doesn't that get lonely?

Claire Lonely is inevitable. At least I'm never bored. What's your map of the world look like?

Jonathan Not nearly as adventurous. I grew up in Margate. I went to RCA – that's the Royal College of Art – and moved here after that. London was a little more affordable back then and this apartment most especially. Between home, halls and these two flats, I've lived in three buildings my entire life. Wow, is that true?
(*Thinks.*) Yeah. Wow.

Claire You're so stable.

Jonathan I think about travelling. I mean, I've travelled. But. I don't know. Picking up and moving somewhere else? I've thought about it. I just . . . I don't know.

Claire Where would you go?

Jonathan Scotland.

Claire Oh, come on . . . think bigger.

Jonathan I've always wanted to go to Finland.

Claire Bigger!

Jonathan Or Vietnam.

Claire That's what I'm talking about, baby! Why don't you go?

Jonathan There's always been something else to do. And the world is just so / scary.

Claire Big.

Silence.

Jonathan How's life at Selfridges?

Claire I met someone today.

Jonathan You always seem to be meeting someone.

Claire Yeah but I think this guy might actually be single.

Jonathan Oh. The other guys aren't? Ed and Phil and Mr Annabel's?

Claire shrugs.

Claire But this boy today was different. First of all, no ring. Which doesn't mean anything I've learned. But he also had this . . . unmarried air about him. Like he still had some hope left in his life. He came in to buy an Hermès scarf for his grandmother's birthday, couldn't you just die? So adorable. Sweet face, but handsome. Blue eyes. Curly, sandy-blonde hair, resolutely in his twenties. A real real boy.

Jonathan What's Real Real Boy's name?

Claire I don't fuckin' know.

Jonathan He didn't tell you his name?

Claire We didn't actually talk.

Jonathan So when you say you 'met' him . . .?

Claire I mean I saw him.

Jonathan smiles.

I'm not crazy, I swear.

Jonathan I didn't say you were.

Claire I know it's not much and I'll probably never see him again. But I saw him today. And he saw me. For like a split second. I think. But he's out there somewhere. He's real. I didn't imagine him. Have you ever seen someone before – maybe on the tube, maybe shopping at Selfridges – and just been utterly captivated by them?

Jonathan stares at her, smiling.

Jonathan Every so often.

Claire That's exactly what happened to me today. He's like a message from the universe telling me not to give up hope, telling me that there are still some real real boys out there. (*She catches herself.*) I know, I'm stupid.

Jonathan No. I think it's . . . (*He chuckles.*)

Claire What?

Jonathan I think it's sweet.

They smile at one another.

Claire And don't pretend you're not as popular with the guys as I am. You know I can hear you fucking from upstairs, right?

Jonathan is instantly mortified.

Jonathan You can?

Claire Oh yes I can.

Jonathan I'm so sorry.

Claire Don't be. I think it's hot. And clearly those boys do, too.

Jonathan Oh God.

Claire I can hear everything that goes on down here. Fucking, cooking, talking. (*Then:*) Crying.

Silence.

Late at night sometimes. I try not to listen, but . . .

Silence.

I'm sorry. I shouldn't have . . . you know what? Forget I said anything.

Silence. The song changes. Something by Johnny Hartman.

It's getting late. I should probably –

Jonathan Do you know this singer?

Claire Um, no.

Jonathan Most people don't. His name is Johnny Hartman. I discovered him at uni. My boyfriend Gabriel introduced me to him.

Claire We like boyfriends like that.

Jonathan Yeah. Gabe was definitely one of those boyfriends. He was American, so you know . . . exotic. He introduced me to so many of my favourite books, movies. Music, most especially. On our first date, he showed me *The Bridges of Madison County*. You know, that old Meryl Streep movie? We watched it in his room and cried like babies.

Claire So gay.

Jonathan Gabe bought the soundtrack, which had a lot of Johnny Hartman on it. We listened to it constantly. After uni, when we moved here together, into your flat. He owned so much vinyl, very retro. Johnny Hartman most of all. Owned all his albums. We were together for over ten years.

Claire Wow. When did you break up?

Jonathan We didn't, actually.

Claire I don't understand. Are you still together?

After a moment:

Jonathan So last year, um, Gabe and I, we'd, ah, we'd been out with some friends this one night. It was late. We were, ah, we were heading to the tube. It was, like, four in the morning. We stopped at a corner shop to get some water. Gabe wanted to stay outside to finish his cigarette. In ten years, I don't think I ever walked into a building with him at the same time. He was always a minute behind me, finishing that fucking cigarette.

Claire Ugh, I know. Isn't that the worst? / I've dated so many smokers, it's –

Jonathan I bought the water and moved to the door and I just saw . . . I wasn't sure, exactly, what it was at first. There were these guys. I don't know where they came from. They were . . .
  Gabe was on the ground. His hands were up, trying to protect his face. Trying to block them, but they were hitting him so hard. In his face. Hitting him. And hitting him. They were kicking him in the stomach. And his chest and ribs. And his face. One of them picked up a brick and they . . .
  I ran out. I don't know what I . . .
  One of them grabbed me by my head and hit me. I fell down. He hit me again. My nose broke. I had blood in my eyes. By the time I'd looked up again, they'd vanished.
  I looked over at Gabe. He was . . . his bottom lip had ripped off. His teeth were gone. His jaw had come unhinged and . . . there was blood everywhere. Gabe's blood.
  I knelt down beside him. He opened his eyes. And he started looking around, frantically. So frightened. I took his hand. I whispered in his ear that I was there, that I was right there with him. His eyes kept darting around, never landing on anything for more than a second. I just kept saying, 'I love you, Gabriel. I love you, Gabriel. I love you, Gabriel.' Then finally, in that moment, he looked at me. Those beautiful brown eyes that I had been gazing into since I was nineteen years old. There, finally, was Gabriel.

He saw me.
And then he died.

A very, very long silence.

Claire I don't even know what to say.

Jonathan That's why they make sympathy cards.

Silence.

Maybe I shouldn't have told you.

Claire Hey baby, too late now.

Jonathan Do you want to see a picture of him?

Claire Oh, I . . .
Sure, yeah. Of course.

He goes to the bedroom and grabs a book from his night stand and returns with it. He opens it and removes a photo and hands it to her.

Jonathan That was Gabriel.

Claire He was handsome.

Jonathan Yes he was.

Silence.

When I hear you upstairs, I sometimes think it's him, walking around.

Claire Maybe he is.

Jonathan I told you I don't believe in ghosts.

Silence.

Claire I feel like either I should stay and we both get blind drunk or I should go now.

Jonathan Don't worry. I'll walk you out.

They move to the door.

Claire Listen, I don't cook.

Jonathan Okay.

Claire I own, like, one plate. It's always dirty.

Jonathan You don't have to reciprocate.

Claire Because I'm not going to. But I'll come back if you invite me again.

Jonathan Then I'll do that.

She kisses him on the cheek.

Claire Thank you. Good night.

Jonathan Night.

She leaves and goes upstairs. He closes the door and moves to the stereo, puts on a new album and then starts to clean.

Jonathan picks up the photo and looks at it. A deep emotion starts to bubble up inside of him. He forces it back down, then tries to clean up, making his way quickly to the bar cart. He pours himself a drink. And then another. And another. He then drinks directly from the bottle.

Jonathan throws on a hoodie and a baseball cap, grabs his phone and leaves the apartment, heading down the stairs and out of the building.

8 BEFORE WORK

The next morning. Claire is getting ready for work. Some music plays, she dances to it as she gets ready. She is in a good mood. She gathers her things and heads out.

Jonathan enters from downstairs, profoundly drunk. Claire leaves her apartment. They meet on the landing.

Claire Good morning! Thank you so much for dinner last – (*Then seeing him.*) Whoa, what happened to you?

Jonathan Late night.

Claire I see that. Where'd you go?

Jonathan Out.

Claire All night?

Jonathan Yeah all night, is that a problem?

Claire Baby, who am I to judge? It just doesn't sound like you, that's all.

Jonathan What do you know about me, Claire? I mean, really, what the fuck do you know about me?

Claire Hey, easy!

He makes his way unsteadily to his apartment.

You need some help?

Jonathan LEAVE ME THE FUCK ALONE!!!

He slams the door violently in her face. He then collapses on the sofa.
Claire knocks at his door. Jonathan doesn't move. She knocks again.

Claire Jonathan? Jonathan, are you okay?
Jonathan, please talk to me.

Nothing.

Look, I know you're . . . I don't know what the word is.
And I know I don't know you, like you said. Not really. But I know you a little. And what little I do know, I like. Do you know that in the six months since I moved to London, you're the first Brit to invite me over for dinner? You don't know what that meant to me. London can be fun but it's a closed shop when it comes to friendships. It's either school chums or family. Foreigners need not apply. And so, you know, I haven't made anything remotely resembling

a real friend here. Not really. And I know the world is big and people are scary and it's safer inside. But it's also lonely inside. And so, I thought, you know, if we're both inside, being safe and lonely, maybe we could be safe and lonely together? I don't know.

Okay. I'm going to go to work now. But I'll be back later to get ready for a date. I can check in on you if you want. Or just, you know, bang on the ceiling and I'll come running.

Okay. Well. Okay.

She waits a moment, then turns to go down the stairs.

9 EARLY FRIDAY NIGHT

Jonathan is at his desk, sketching.

Claire comes home from work in a mad rush. She bounds up the stairs, taking them two at a time. As she passes Jonathan's apartment, he looks up. She clip-clops across the floor to her bedroom. He goes back to the table, looks up at the ceiling, then continues sketching.

She tears out of her work clothes, changes her bra and underwear, reapplies some deodorant and then madly rummages through her closet. She tosses a handful of dresses onto her air mattress, sifting through them. She finally lands on the one she wants to wear and quickly slips into it. She starts kicking a few shoe boxes around the room until the shoes fall out and she finds the pair she wants, slipping them on.

She changes her earrings, necklace and bracelet. She sprays some perfume then dashes out of the room and then makes a sudden about-face and heads back to the bedroom.

Claire Listen to Coco, Claire. Listen to Coco.

She ditches the bracelet and then heads back to the door. She grabs her things and goes. Jonathan looks up as she passes his door.

Jonathan Claire?

But she's gone. He goes back to his work.

10 LATE SATURDAY NIGHT

Jonathan is asleep. It is raining outside.

Downstairs, the front door opens. The clip-clop of Claire's shoes echoes across the lobby and then she enters up the stairs, drenched. If that weren't bad enough, her dress is ripped at the shoulder and one of her heels is broken.

She is shaky, carefully negotiating each step. She gets to Jonathan's door and stops, hesitates a moment, then knocks. Then knocks harder and faster.

Jonathan wakes up and comes to the door.

Jonathan Hello?

Claire Jonathan? It's me.

Jonathan Claire?

He opens the door, taking in the sight of her.

Claire Hey.

Jonathan Are you okay?

Claire Can I borrow some money for a cab?

Jonathan What?

Claire Please?

Jonathan What time is it?

Claire Five thirty?

Jonathan Jesus, Claire.

Claire I'm sorry to wake you, I . . . don't have any cash and he's waiting.

He rifles through a drawer and pulls out some money.

Can you, ah . . . It's just that my heel's broken . . . (*She points to her broken shoe.*)

I'll pay you back, I promise.

He throws on a coat and rushes downstairs.

Your shoes! Put on some . . .

He's gone.

. . . shoes.

She looks around for a moment, then hobbles inside. After a few moments, Jonathan returns.

Thank you.

Jonathan Are you okay?

Claire I'll be fine.

Jonathan What happened?

Claire Ah, well, things . . . things got a little rough.

Jonathan What happened?

Claire Just a few bumps and bruises is all. I'll be fine.

Jonathan Please tell me what happened.

Claire Mr Finance Bro. I don't know if I told you about him or not.

Jonathan I can't keep track of them all.

Claire Neither can I. Anyway, Mr Finance Bro is this guy from New York, we see each other whenever we're in the same town. He always knows the best new restaurants and clubs and he's, like, stupidly handsome. He's just a fun night out, you know?

Jonathan Okay . . .

Claire Anyway, tonight . . . we're in the back of an Uber headed to some new bar in Shoreditch and he starts stroking my leg. I guess I just wasn't in the mood for it and so I asked him to stop. He laughed, I guess thinking I was joking, and he kept on doing it. So then I told him to stop, physically removing his hand from my leg. He did not like that. Told me to get the fuck out of the car, which would have been fine except we were in Shoreditch and my phone was, as always, dead. So I told him no, I wouldn't get out of the car unless he gave me some money for a taxi home.

Jonathan Okay . . .

Claire So he goes, 'What do I look like, you stupid cunt? A fuckin' ATM machine?'

Jonathan Jesus.

Claire And so I say, '"ATM machine' is redundant, you asshole. It's just "ATM".' He really didn't like that. He tells the Uber driver to stop, reaches over and opens my door and shoves me out onto the street.

Jonathan Oh Claire, I'm so sorry.

Claire He ripped my dress, which, by the way, I now own, thanks a lot, Mr Asshole Finance Bro. I'm screaming at him that I have no money, no way of getting home, no anything.

Jonathan (*concerned, not scolding*) Oh, Claire . . .

Claire And then he slams the door and the car speeds away. Bye-bye, Bro.

Jonathan What did you do?

Claire I walked!

Jonathan From Shoreditch?

Claire What else was I going to do? All the way home. In three-inch heels, Jesus. Well, I'm exaggerating a little. Up Kingsland Road until it becomes Stoke Newington Road, soaked and freezing my ass off. I would've walked all the way but then my heel. I thought it only happened in the movies. Twenty-nine years on this planet – a third of that in heels – and I've never had one break on me. Tonight, of course. So I hailed a taxi, begged him to take me home. And then I woke you. And I'm sorry.

He grabs a blanket and wraps it around her shoulders.

I bet you Real Real Boy doesn't do that to women. I bet you Real Real Boy hangs out in better places than Shoreditch. He came back in again. Didn't buy anything. Just talked to me for a bit and left.

Jonathan You deserve a Real Real Boy.

She snuggles up next to him.

Are you happy, Claire?

Claire You kidding me? My dress is ripped, my make-up's running, my / hair's all fucked up.

Jonathan I mean, in general. Big-picture happy.

Claire Big picture? Who knows, man? I try not to think about it too much. It just depresses me.

Jonathan I want to be happy. I really, really do. I just don't seem to know how any more.

Claire Baby, if I knew, I promise I wouldn't keep it from you.

Jonathan Maybe it's this city. Maybe somewhere else is better.

Claire I've been there. It's not.

Jonathan Maybe I should be like you and move every year or so.

Claire It's hell on the luggage.

Jonathan Gabe and I used to dream of moving out to the country. The Cotswolds. A farmhouse away from the world.

Claire Who are the Cotswolds?

Jonathan It's a where, not a who. We'd wake up every morning, get the kids off to school. Packed lunches. I'm good at those.

Claire I believe that.

Jonathan I go to work and Gabe paints in his studio somewhere near the house. The kids come home. One of us cooks, the other helps with homework. Dinner, story time, bed time, 'us' time.

Claire That sounds really nice.

Jonathan Johnny Hartman playing on an endless loop. Easter and Guy Fawkes and / Christmas.

Claire Christmas.

Jonathan And so much love. Our whole life wrapped up in this fantasy for the future. They were so modest, our dreams. So perfectly sized.

Claire Would there be a fireplace?

Jonathan There'd be three. And a stream that flowed right by the house that you could hear from every room.

Claire And snow on the ground in the winter.

Jonathan And blazing red leaves in the autumn.

Claire And wildflowers in the summer.

Jonathan And so much love.

Silence.

Do you want to, um . . .

Claire What?

Jonathan Stay here tonight?
Sleep here?
You could stay here if you wanted.

I used to play with Gabe's hair as he drifted off to sleep. He'd have trouble falling asleep sometimes. It's a nice way to fall asleep.

Claire I'd like that.

Jonathan Just for tonight?

Claire Thank you.

He holds out his hand. She takes it. He leads her to the bedroom and then gets into bed. She stands there a moment, then takes off her dress and lays it over a chair. She crawls into bed next to him. Hesitantly, he wraps his arms around her.

Jonathan Thank you.

He holds her in his arms.

Act Two

1 BEFORE WORK

A transformation. Instead of the overstuffed, pack-rat apartment from before, Jonathan's place is now neat and orderly. The mountains of books have been trimmed down to what fits on the shelves. The paperwork has been brought to order. His art supplies have disappeared. Several extraneous pieces of furniture are gone. His bedroom is uncluttered and the bed is made. And most noticeably: Gabe's paintings are gone, replaced by vintage movie and National Gallery posters. It is a much more calming place to be.

A transformation has occurred upstairs as well, although on a much more modest scale. The empty bottles and take-out boxes are gone. The kitchen is now sterile and spotless. There is a little more order to Claire's bedroom, although the bed is still perennially unmade. But far fewer clothes litter the space and her vanity has been brought into some kind of order. Most significantly, one of Gabe's paintings now graces the once bare bedroom wall.

At rise, Radio 4 plays. Both apartments are empty. We stay here a moment, allowing ourselves to look at the apartments for a moment, noticing the changes, listening to the news.

Then Jonathan bounds up the stairs from the lobby in a pair of pyjamas and a robe, a copy of the Guardian.

Jonathan climbs the stairs to his landing, calling up to Claire's apartment:

Jonathan You're gonna be late!

Claire (*from the bathroom*) No I'm not!

> *Jonathan continues into his apartment, leaving the door open. He goes to the kitchen to pour himself a cup of*

coffee. He then holds the plastic wrapper upside-down, allowing the paper to fall to the table. He grabs the main section and heads with it and his coffee to the sofa. He hits the radio on his way over, turning it off. He then settles in to read the paper.

Claire comes out of the bathroom in work clothes, face done up for the day. She grabs her coat and bag and heads down to this apartment.

Morning!

Jonathan (*not looking up*) Good morning.

Claire Coffee ready?

Jonathan points toward the kitchen. Claire heads there.

Jonathan You're gonna be late.

Claire I've got plenty of time.

Claire pours herself a cup of coffee, then helps herself to some oat milk from the fridge.

You're almost out of oat milk.

Jonathan Roger that.

Claire You're the only person I know who still reads the print edition of the *Guardian*.

Jonathan I'm the only person you know who reads.

Claire You know that one of these days they're going to stop printing it altogether.

Jonathan All the more reason to enjoy it while I can.

Claire Why did you buy that Kindle if you're never going to use it?

Jonathan I'm working up to it, don't rush me. It's nice to sit with the paper in the morning. Preferably in silence.

Claire Oh come on, Jonathan.

Jonathan I just saw you eight hours ago and all you've done since then is sleep. Literally nothing has happened to you since I last laid eyes on you. But a lot has gone on in the world. This (*the paper*) catches me up on all those things as you have nothing new to report.

Claire I had a sex dream about Suella Braverman.

Jonathan You did not.

Claire Wouldn't that have been amazing, though?

Jonathan Not for Suella. Or you, for that matter.

She joins him on the sofa.

Claire Morning, grumpy.

Jonathan You're going to be late for work.

Claire I've got plenty of time. Hey, is there any of that yummy sourdough left?

Jonathan Should be.

Claire heads to the kitchen, finds the bread, takes out the toaster and puts two slices in. While this happens:

Claire What are your plans today?

Jonathan I thought I'd finish the paper if you'll let me.

Claire Blah blah.

Jonathan Then do a little laundry / maybe read for a –

Claire Ooh, could you do some for me / if I left it in the hall?

Jonathan Leave it in the hall on your way out.

Claire Thank you!

Jonathan Then, I don't know. Clean up the mess you're making in the kitchen. Maybe some online Christmas shopping.

Claire I keep a very robust Amazon wish list.

Jonathan So you've told me every single day since Halloween.

Claire You think you might get to a grocery store today?

Jonathan I dunno, why?

Claire Just the oat milk.

Jonathan I'll do an Ocado order.

Claire When was the last time you left this apartment, Jonathan?

Jonathan I don't know, Claire. I don't keep track. Why? Do you?

Claire It's been a few days.

Jonathan It's cold.

Claire It's December.

Jonathan Yeah, so . . .

Claire Christmastime. You love Christmas.

Jonathan I used to. It's gotten so commercialised.

Claire Of course Christmas is commercialised. That's what makes it so awesome. Who wants a non-commercialised Christmas? What even is that? Church and Advent candles and fucking Yule logs? No, you want *Home Alone*, Mariah Carey, and rank, shameless commercialism.

She looks for a response but he just makes a point of delving deeper into his paper. After a moment:

Claire Oh come on, Jonathan!

Jonathan Okay, you wanna talk? Let's talk.

Claire Yes! What should we talk about?

Jonathan Well, speaking of Christmas, I was actually thinking / about what we –

Claire I was too! Let's share our thoughts at the same time.

Jonathan Okay. You ready?

Claire Yes. One, two, three.
We should get a tree!

Jonathan We should spend Christmas in the Cotswolds.
Mine was longer. I didn't hear yours.

Claire The Cotswolds?

Jonathan I was thinking. But wait, what was your idea?

Claire That we get a tree.

Jonathan I think my idea is better.

Claire You want to go to the Cotswolds?

Jonathan I was thinking we could rent a house for Christmas.

Claire I can't afford that.

Jonathan It'll be my present to you.

Claire No, Jonathan, that's too extravagant.

Jonathan I have money saved.

Claire Yeah, to live off of, not take holidays at peak travel times. Oh my God, Jonathan. Do you hear the words that are coming out of my mouth? *I'm* being the voice of moderation here. Doesn't that tell you something?

Jonathan We'll look for a place with a nice big fireplace. Wouldn't that be nice? Quietly reading in front of the fire. Well, me reading and you talking to me. Maybe bring some movies. You still have never seen *Casablanca*. Let's go away and have some peace and quiet. Breathe clean air. Rest our brains. Somewhere sa— (*He catches himself.*) Somewhere serene.

Pause.

Claire Yes.

Jonathan Yeah?

Claire Yes, absolutely! I would love to.

Jonathan Great. It'll be amazing. And you are definitely going to be late for work.

Claire I'm not going to be – (*She sees the time.*) Holy shit, is that the time?!? Fuck I'm gonna be late!

She scrambles up and grabs her coat and bag.

Jonathan You're definitely down with this Cotswolds idea, though, yes? / Because I'm going to start looking, if so.

Claire Yes! I think it's splendid, Jonathan, I really do. Thank you. You're the greatest guy I've ever met in my entire life.

Jonathan Am I your favourite in the whole wide world?

Claire Topnumberonefirstbest! Look for a place with a hot tub!

She exits the building. Jonathan stands there, smiling. He then grabs his coffee and Claire's uneaten toast and moves back to his newspaper. He reads for a moment, then puts the paper down. He grabs his new Kindle off the shelf and starts clicking through it, attempting to read off it, giving it a serious go. After a few moments, he tosses it aside and picks up the paper again. Then he looks around his apartment. It's as if he doesn't really know what to do by himself. Fear creeps in. His loneliness returns full force.

A moment, then he gives up on the paper and goes to his computer. A few clicks and then the sound of a porn starts up. He watches for a moment, eventually sliding his hands down his pyjama bottoms and starts to stroke himself.

2 LATE AT NIGHT

Both Jonathan and Claire are asleep in their beds. Jonathan jerks awake with a cry. He's drenched in sweat and panting. It takes him a second or two to realise he's safe, that he's just had a bad dream.

Jonathan throws off the covers and sits on the edge of the bed, trying to recover from the dream. He then moves into the kitchen, pouring himself a glass of water.

Jonathan grabs his broom. He heads with it into the bedroom and reaches up with it and bangs it on his ceiling. One-two-three. One-two-three. He waits. Nothing from Claire. Again, this time a little harder. One-two-three. One-two-three.

Claire awakes, reaches over and knocks on her floor. One-two.

Jonathan puts the broom away and unlocks his apartment door, heads back to the bedroom and climbs back into bed. As he does this, Claire gets out of bed and pads over to her apartment door, half asleep. She totters down the stairs and onto his landing, opening the door she knows will be unlocked for her.

Claire pads her way into Jonathan's bedroom. Jonathan pulls the covers open for her and she slips in. He wraps his arms around her and they sleep.

3 BEFORE WORK

Early morning. Jonathan and Claire are asleep in Jonathan's bed. The alarm goes off. They stir awake.

Claire What time is it?

Jonathan Seven thirty.

Claire Why so early?

Jonathan Time waits for no man.

Claire Well, I'm a woman, so let me sleep.

Jonathan This is why you're always late for work.

She ignores him and tries to go back to sleep. He nudges her.

Claire.

Nothing.

Come on, Claire. Get up.

She still ignores him. He then 'attacks' her, grabbing her and wrapping her in his arms, pulling her on top of him, her back to his front. He roars and growls like a monster. Claire instantly starts to laugh. It's all very playful.

Claire No, quit it! I'm up! I'm up.

Jonathan Too late! You must be tickled now.

Claire No! No, don't tickle me, Jonathan, no!

They wrestle and play fight, laughing as they do. Then her hand accidentally grazes his cock, which is fully erect. She responds with surprise.

Oh! Oh God, that's your penis!

Jonathan Jesus, I'm so sorry. My morning wood is kind of aggressive.

She peeks under the covers.

Claire Dude, you're hung.

Jonathan Don't look at my penis.

Claire Well, don't wave it in my face.

Jonathan I didn't.

Claire Christ, no wonder you have those boys moaning.

Jonathan Shut up about my penis!

A beat, then she snuggles up next to him, resting her head on his chest. He wraps his arm around her.

Claire Your bed is so comfortable.

Jonathan I love this bed.

Claire That air mattress is slowly destroying my back.

Jonathan You should get a real bed.

Claire I've travelled the world with that air mattress. She's my best friend, even if she's trying to kill me.

She turns on her side, facing away from him.

Spoon me for five minutes, then I promise I'll get up.

Jonathan turns and envelops her in his arms and spoons her.

So was it another dream last night? Is that why you –

Jonathan Yeah.

Claire You wanna talk about it?

Pause.

Jonathan We'll sleep better in the Cotswolds.

4 AFTER WORK

Another evening. Christmas music plays on Jonathan's stereo as he packs for the Cotswolds. Upstairs, Claire's suitcases are packed for the trip. She's bringing far more than she needs.

Claire comes home from work. She carries a small Selfridges bag. She clip-clops up the stairs. Jonathan hears and rushes over to the door and bounds out into the hall.

Jonathan Hey, come in here for a second. I have a treat for you.

Claire Okay, let me run upstairs and change first.

Jonathan It'll take just a second. Come on.

He grabs her and drags her into the apartment. She tries to hide her shopping bag.

Close your eyes.

Claire Oh boy!

She does. Jonathan goes to the kitchen and takes a baking sheet off the counter and brings it to her. It is filled with row after row of perfectly made gingerbread cookies.

Jonathan Okay, open them.

She does, sees the cookies, gasps.

Claire No way! You made these?

Jonathan Merry Christmas.

Claire They're beautiful! I thought Christmas was too commercialised.

Jonathan It is but I stopped caring.

Claire That's the spirit!

Jonathan I made them to bring to the Cotswolds. Try one.

Claire I'll have one after dinner.

Jonathan I also ordered some amazing cheeses on Ocado. And there's an amazing butcher about twenty minutes from where we're staying. I figured we could swing by on our way up and get a couple of steaks and even maybe some meat for stew if they have some.

Claire Let me run upstairs and change and I'll come back down in a minute.

Jonathan You know I can see that bag in your hand.

Claire Oh –

Jonathan Is that my Christmas present?

He grabs for it. She avoids again.

Claire No.

He grabs again, she runs away.

Jonathan I wanna see.

Claire No. Just leave it.

Jonathan Oh come on. You already know what your present is.

Claire Jonathan, no, it's –

He gets the bag and pulls out an orange Hermès box.

Jonathan Whoa.

Claire Just, give it here.

Jonathan Hermès! Even I know what that is.

Claire Just –

Jonathan You bought me something from Hermès?

Claire No.

He opens the box and pulls out a gorgeous silk scarf.

Jonathan You bought me a . . . what is this?

Claire It's not for you.

Jonathan I don't understand. Who's it for?

Claire It's for me.

Jonathan Don't tell me you 'borrowed' this.

Claire No. It was given to me.

Jonathan By who?

No answer.

What's with the mystery, Claire?

She takes it from him and returns it to the box.

Claire Real Real Boy gave it to me.

Silence.

Jonathan Real Real Boy is back?

Claire He's been in a lot recently.

Jonathan You didn't tell me that.

Claire It didn't seem relevant. Anyway, he was browsing, just like always and I was helping him, just like always. He was looking at scarves again and he asked me which one I liked best. Of course, I picked out the most expensive one. He paid for it, had me box it up and put it in the bag for him. I handed it to him and then he handed it back to me and said, 'Merry Christmas. This is for you.'

Pause.

Jonathan Wow.

Claire And then he said, 'I've spent the last two months working up the courage to do that.'

Jonathan He said that?

Claire Yeah, so . . .

Jonathan So wow. Merry Christmas, indeed.

Claire Merry Christmas.

Pause.

He asked me out.

Jonathan Real Real Boy?

Claire Yeah. Marcus.

Jonathan Oh. Well, yeah. Of course. Of course Marcus did.

Claire He wants to take me to River Cafe.

Jonathan Look at you.

Silence.

I haven't even thought about dinner tonight. What do you think about ordering some pizza?

Claire Are you upset?

Jonathan Why would I be upset?

Claire I don't know, that's why I'm asking.

Jonathan I'm happy for you, Claire.

Claire The thing is, um, he's away the rest of the week and he gets back Saturday afternoon.

Jonathan That's the day we leave for the Cotswolds.

Claire Yeah.

Jonathan So . . .

Claire So I was thinking, I was thinking maybe we could postpone our trip by one day? We're there for so long, I figured . . .

Pause.

I can tell him no.

Jonathan Don't be silly. Go on your date.

Claire Are you sure?

Jonathan Yup.

Silence.

In fact, we don't even have to go to the Cotswolds if you don't want to.

Claire Of course I want to.

Jonathan Maybe I'll just drive down on Saturday and you can take the train whenever you feel like it.

Claire Hey, Jonathan, come on.

Jonathan Or maybe you and Marcus can go together instead and I'll just stay here. How's that sound?

Claire Don't be such a fucking child.

Jonathan Do whatever you want, Claire. You always do.

Claire Hey!

Jonathan This is so typical of you.

Claire It's one night! We can leave first thing Sunday morning!

Jonathan Just be sure to rinse Marcus's cum out of your mouth first.

A beat, then:

Claire Fuck you.

She storms out of the apartment, slamming the door behind her, trudging up the stairs loudly. She gets to her apartment and lets herself in and slams that door behind her, too. She goes to her room and undresses, walking naked to her bathroom. She closes the door. We hear the shower start to run.

While this is happening, Jonathan grabs a vodka bottle from the freezer and starts chugging. He sits on his bed, fuming, drinking.

5 SATURDAY NIGHT

In Jonathan's apartment, several more bags are packed. There are also several canvas M&S bags filled with groceries. His buzzer goes off. He goes to it.

Jonathan Hello?

Voice on Intercom Delivery.

He buzzes the delivery person in and runs downstairs to meet them. He re-enters carrying a garment bag. He gets to his landing, faces the stairs leading up to Claire's apartment. He takes a moment, then quickly ascends. He pauses at the top of the stairs. This is the furthest upstairs he's ever gone in the play. He feels a lot, being back up here. He takes it all in, being at the doorway to his old apartment with Gabe. Memories flood into his mind. He then hangs the garment bag from the top of the door frame, knocks on the door and rushes downstairs to his apartment.
Claire emerges from her bathroom, wearing a robe. Her hair and make-up all done up.

Claire Hello?

Claire goes to her door and opens it. She is surprised by the garment bag. She takes it down and looks into the hallway.

Jonathan?

Claire goes back inside and unzips the bag to reveal a gorgeous, elegant designer dress. The kind she wouldn't ever dare to borrow, let alone be able to afford. She removes the bag and takes the dress off the door frame, holding it out to look at it. It is pure beauty. She is overwhelmed. She immediately takes off her robe and tries the dress on. It is a stunner. This dress is your first kiss, a dream come true, a take-your-breath-away once-in-a-lifetime dress. She looks at herself in a mirror and is transfixed by how gorgeous she looks.
On Jonathan's stereo, Johnny Hartman starts singing 'I See Your Face Before Me'.
Claire leaves her apartment and comes down the stairs to Jonathan's. She knocks. He opens the door. They stare at each other a moment.

Jonathan I'm sorry.

Claire Most people just buy a card.

Jonathan They didn't have one in your size.

She melts.

Claire You really shouldn't have.

Jonathan Yes, in fact, it seems I absolutely should.

Claire How do I look?

She spins.

Jonathan You look . . . wow. Marcus is a lucky man to have you on his arm tonight.
Come in.

She does, instantly recognising the music. She smiles.

Claire Johnny Hartman.

Jonathan Very good.
How does it fit?

Claire You tell me.

Jonathan Like a dream.

Claire I wish my dreams were this good. Where did you get it?

Jonathan I found it online. I was so afraid it wouldn't fit. Do you like it?

Claire I'm going to wear this every day for the rest of my life. I feel like I'm going to the prom or something. But, you know, in Monaco.

Jonathan I wanted you to feel . . . how I see you.

He holds out his hands for her. She takes them. He spins her. The dress performs a pyrotechnic display of grace and beauty.

Will you still come with me to the Cotswolds?

Claire Yes. Yes, of course I will. I'll pack my bag as soon as I get home tonight and we can leave first thing in the morning. I would love nothing more.

Jonathan looks at her.

Jonathan You look so beautiful.

She spins again.

Claire I love doing that. I've never had a dress that did that before. I think I'll do it again.

She spins once again.

Jonathan That dress was made to be danced in.

Claire Maybe we should go out and do that one night. You, me and Princess Grace here.

Jonathan The only places I know to go dancing, that dress would be ruined.

Claire We'll find someplace elegant and fancy. Those places still exist, don't they? One miserable night in February. We'll get dolled up – maybe buy you a new suit – and we'll dance until the sun rises. Can you dance?

Jonathan I did ballet for a few months at uni.

Claire That is / so SWEET!

Jonathan Don't say it.

She holds out her arms for him. He hesitates, then reaches out, first for her fingers, then up her arms, finally pulling her into a close embrace. They look deeply into each other's eyes.

They dance. The song is hypnotic. There is real intimacy between them. Take your time with this. More time than you think you need. She rests her head on his chest, he smells her hair, then kisses her temple. After a moment, she lifts her head and looks up at him. Then, cautiously, fearfully, achingly, they kiss. It is a deep, prolonged, real real kiss. The song ends. They pull apart. Electricity between them. Claire's phone beeps with a text message alert. It rudely breaks the spell. They don't want to pull away. Finally, they do. She goes to her phone and checks it.

Claire He's in a car, coming to pick me up. He's almost here. I should probably finish getting ready.

Jonathan Yeah.

He follows her to the door and stands there, his hand on the doorknob. She stands on the other side of the door, her hand on the doorknob, as well. They stay in this moment a few seconds, then she runs back up to her apartment, grabs her coat and checks herself one last time in the mirror. She is entranced by the dress. She looks down at the floor, at Jonathan's apartment, then back up at herself. While this is happening, Jonathan pours himself a drink. He sits in his apartment, shaken by what has occurred. He drinks.

A moment, then Jonathan's buzzer goes off. He jumps at the sound. It goes off again. He moves to the buzzer and presses the button.

Hey, um, wrong flat. She's upstairs.

Over the buzzer, we hear the muffled sound of a man's voice saying, 'Oh, I, um –' and then Jonathan buzzes him in without hearing the rest. Jonathan pours another drink.

The door opens downstairs and footsteps are heard crossing the lobby, then climbing the stairs. As they get closer, we see who it is:
Wes.
He comes up to Jonathan's landing, then moves over to the door, takes a breath and knocks.
Jonathan moves to the door and as he does:

Hey, um, she's one flight up.

He opens the door and gets quite the surprise. They stare at each other a second.

Wes Hi.

Jonathan continues to stare, dumbfounded.

Is this a bad time?

No response from Jonathan.

I was just, you know, in the neighbourhood. Well, obviously, right? Oh! I have your book!

Jonathan Wes . . .

Wes digs in his bag.

Wes Yeah. Sorry. I was walking home from the bus and I saw your lights were on and I figured I'd run home and grab it and bring it over. I told you I'd return it.

Jonathan You didn't have to do that.

Wes I know but . . . I read it and . . . it's . . . exactly like you said. I read it twice, actually. I just . . . couldn't help myself. I think it may have changed my life.

Jonathan Wes . . .

Wes I just wanted to . . . tell you that. I loved everything about it.

Jonathan I'm glad. Look –

Wes I had a question for you, though. It's on page 396. There was a passage you'd underlined. Here . . .

Wes holds the book open to page 396 and an underlined passage.

It's the only passage in the book you underlined. Why this one?

Jonathan I don't remember.

Wes You must have really understood the feeling he was describing. Maybe you don't any more, I don't know. But there was a time you were so moved by that sentence that you grabbed a pen and underlined it. What was the word you used to describe what it feels like to read a book? Physically, I mean. You said it was . . . what? Tangible? No, ah . . . tactile! Yes! Tactile. Right.

Jonathan Listen, I'm really / not –

Wes (*offering the book to Jonathan*) Look: you can run your fingers over the other side of the page and feel the indentation your pen made. See?

Jonathan takes the book and feels the pen mark.

That indentation says, 'Jonathan was here. Jonathan felt this.' Do you see that?

Am I . . . ? I don't know if I'm making any . . . all I really want to say is I think I discovered another reason why books are superior to Kindles and I just wanted to share that with you. This pen mark.

Where were you when you underlined that sentence?
Do you still own that pen?
Anyway, you can see how my mind works, right?

Pause.

So . . . whatcha been up to?

Jonathan Wes, this isn't really a good / time.

Wes Oh . . . oh, I'm / sorry.

Jonathan It's just that –

Wes You're busy.

Jonathan Now's not a good time.

Wes I understand. I was just hoping – I don't know, it's silly, I guess – I was just hoping maybe we could – I thought I'd take a chance and – maybe it was a mistake. I'm . . . I'm sorry. I'll just, ah, I'll see you around.

Wes makes an abrupt move toward the stairs. Jonathan struggles for what to say. Wes is almost gone when:

Jonathan You just took me by surprise is all.

Wes *(off)* Good surprise or bad surprise?

Jonathan I don't know, really.

Wes *(off)* So is now still not a good time?

Jonathan looks up at Claire's apartment.

Jonathan Maybe for just a minute.

A moment, then Wes suddenly comes bounding up the stairs, taking them three at a time. TRYING SO HARD to keep his cool but it's just not happening. Jonathan ushers Wes in. Jonathan picks up his drink.

Upstairs, Claire's buzzer goes off. She jumps at the sound. She gathers her things, then walks to the door, then steps out into the hallway. She stands there a long moment, willing herself to go down the stairs but she can't seem to. She only gets a step or two, then looks down at Jonathan's door. She then tiptoes back into her apartment. She moves to her camping chair and sits.

Wes Whoa! This place has changed.

Jonathan Oh, yeah.

Wes Wait, what happened to your books?

Jonathan I . . . I got rid of a lot of them.

Wes But . . . Jonathan! You . . . that's . . . why?

Jonathan Just streamlining.

Wes What did you do with them?

Jonathan I gave them to Oxfam.

Wes I would have taken them!

Jonathan I thought you were devoted to your Kindle!

Wes Did you not hear the big speech I just made out in the hall?

Jonathan There's still a lot left.

Claire's buzzer goes off again. She gets up and paces around, freaking out, trying to decide what to do. She moves to the window and looks down, careful not to be seen.

Wes Weren't there paintings on the wall last time?

Jonathan Oh, I –

Wes There were, weren't there?

Jonathan Yeah, I, um, I got rid of those, too.

Wes What is happening to you, Jonathan?

Jonathan Do you want a drink?

Wes No thanks, I'm a lightweight.

Wes notices the suitcase and canvas shopping bags.

Are you going on a trip?

Jonathan Yeah, for Christmas.

Wes Where are you going?

Jonathan The Cotswolds, with a friend.

Wes Oh. Oh, a 'friend'.

Jonathan No, not like that. Just a friend.

Wes continues to look around.

Wes It does look better in here.

Jonathan It's easier to think in here now.

Wes Yeah, I get that. Calming.

Jonathan Yeah.

Wes continues to look around, then spots the Kindle. He picks it up in disbelief.

Wes What's the meaning of this bullshit?!?

Jonathan Oh. I never use it, I promise. I don't even know how to turn it on.

Wes I got rid of mine because of you.

Jonathan You didn't.

Wes Of course I did, you were very persuasive. Bloody hell, it's like you convert me to your religion and then lose your own faith.

Jonathan I promise that I'm still the same Luddite I always was.

Wes Did you change the bedroom? Can I see?

Jonathan There's . . . not really any –

Wes moves to the bedroom.

Wes The scene of the crime.
Do you ever think about . . .? Never mind.

Jonathan That night?

Wes Yeah.

Jonathan Sometimes.

Wes You do?

Jonathan Yeah.

Wes Like fleeting thought or wank fantasy?

Jonathan Both.

Wes Really?

Jonathan Yeah.

Wes Cool. Me too.

Beat.

What was your favourite part?
  Mine was when you picked me up and I was facing you, like . . . riding you, but also completely supported by you, you know?

Jonathan I think.

Wes You were holding my arse and I was holding on to your neck and shoulders.

Jonathan Right.

Wes Yeah.
  Anyway.

Wes sits on the bed. Silence.
  Claire's buzzer goes off again. She stands stock-still, looks at herself and her beautiful dress in the mirror and begins to cry.

Jonathan Listen, I should really / get back –

Wes Am I just totally barking up the wrong tree here?

Jonathan I don't –

Wes It's just that you always seem to be in a rush to get rid of me.

Jonathan Always? I've met you once.

Wes And whose fault is that? Are you seeing someone?

Jonathan Ah . . . no.

Wes What's that 'ah' for?

Jonathan What do you mean?

Wes You had to think.

Jonathan No, it was just an 'ah'.

Wes An 'ah' of thought?

Jonathan An 'ah' of discomfort.

Wes Oh God, am I making you / uncomfortable?

Jonathan Wes?

Wes Yeah?

Jonathan Stop talking.

Wes Okay.

Silence.

Jonathan There's no one in my . . . I have no one.

Claire's phone rings. She hits 'ignore'. She then powers down the phone and goes into her bedroom and takes the dress off. She hangs it up in the closet, then puts her robe back on and collapses onto the air mattress and curls up into a ball, burying her head under a pillow.

Wes It feels that way sometimes, doesn't it?

Jonathan What?

Wes You said, 'I have no one.'

Jonathan I didn't mean / that I have –

Wes I know but still. It feels that way. I think maybe that's what Baldwin was writing about. You know what I mean?

Jonathan I'm not sure that I –

Wes Having people in your life but still not feeling connected to anything. Never alone but still somehow lonely.

Jonathan Right.

Wes Do you feel that way, too?

Jonathan I understand that, yeah.

Wes But do you feel it?

> *Beat.*

Jonathan Yes.

Wes So it's not just me?

Jonathan No.

> *Wes smiles.*

Wes I don't understand . . . how I'm supposed to . . . like, integrate. Do you know what I mean? I go to bars but everyone already has their group. Or if they're not in a group, they've got their faces in their phones.

Jonathan Yeah.

Wes I thought coming to London would be like uni but even better. It's more like secondary school but even worse. How are you supposed to meet people?

Jonathan We met.

Wes On Grindr. For sex. And afterwards you kicked me out and haven't spoken to me since.

Jonathan And yet here you are.

Wes So stalking people. This is your advice?

Jonathan Are you stalking me?

Wes Um . . . no?

Jonathan Maybe London isn't your town.

Wes Maybe. Is it yours?

Jonathan I don't know any more.

Wes Let's move somewhere together!

Jonathan Ah . . .

Wes That was an 'ah' of discomfort, definitely.

Jonathan Yes.

Wes I know I'm way into overtime with you right now . . .

Jonathan I'm not watching the clock.

Wes There's something I want you to know about the night we met.

This scares Jonathan.

Jonathan Okay?

Wes That night . . . um . . . that night was my birthday.

This actually moves Jonathan quite a bit.

Jonathan Oh, Wes.

Wes Yeah. Well, so, I didn't have plans, right? Well, I did but my 'friends' bailed on me at the last minute. And by 'bailed' I mean no one showed up at the bar I said I'd be at after work.

Jonathan Oh, Wes, I'm so / sorry.

Wes Whatever, it's fine. So I came home and I went on Grindr. And Scruff. And Feeld. All three at once. Like mission control. I just wanted to . . . I dunno . . . I just wanted someone to notice me. Pathetic, right?

Jonathan No.

Wes Maybe a little?

Jonathan I feel it, too.

Wes You do?

Jonathan nods.

Then you said hi. And it wasn't just a 'hey' or a ''sup?' It was a proper hello. You asked me about my day. And I almost told you it was my birthday. But then I thought you'd think I was pathetic for being on Grindr on my birthday and not out with friends and so I didn't say anything. We talked about movies. And how much we both loved autumn. And then we realised we lived a short walk from each other. And you asked me if I liked whisky and I said yes, even though I hate whisky. And then you invited me over. And I was so nervous.

Jonathan I could tell.

Wes Were you nervous?

Jonathan I was, yes.

Wes I couldn't tell.

Jonathan The whisky, maybe.

Wes Maybe. And I thought, 'This guy is way too fit for me. He's not going to want to fuck me.'

Jonathan inadvertently moves his hand toward Wes, gently and innocently touching his leg.

Jonathan You're beautiful, Wes.

Beat.

Wes Really?

Jonathan Yes.

Wes Thank you.

Wes takes Jonathan's hand in his. Wes smiles. Jonathan then gently withdraws his hand.

And then you excused yourself and went to the bathroom and I thought for a moment of just leaving. But then you came back out and you kissed me and I could –

Wes stops himself.

Jonathan What?

Wes Your eyes were wet. You'd been crying in the bathroom. Right?

Pause.

Jonathan Yes.

Wes Why?

Jonathan That, um . . . that's . . .

Wes Not a story for tonight?

Jonathan Probably not.

Wes Anyway, I didn't say anything because I didn't want to embarrass you but it made me, I don't know, comfortable. For some reason. It made me feel safe. And then to have you hold me. To be held, really held, it's . . . it's my favourite thing, I think. And then to come in here, to this bed. How you were so gentle with me. Like I was this fragile thing. Which I was. But how could you know that? And then how you fucked me. Oh God, how you fucked me. It was amazing. It truly, truly was.

Silence. Then . . .

It was, wasn't it?

Jonathan Yes. It was.

Wes Oh, good. Yes. And, I don't know, everything just disappeared for a while. I didn't feel pathetic, like the boy who got stood up by his so-called friends on his birthday. I didn't feel lonely. I felt, well, special.

Jonathan I know what you / mean.

Wes And I got home and I realised that only an hour had passed. I felt as though my life had changed, here in your apartment. How could all that have happened in only an hour? It didn't seem possible. And of course it wasn't. It was still my birthday and I was still alone. I just wanted that special feeling back. And so . . . I went back on Grindr. And eventually some other guy said hello. And I went back out. And I got fucked again.

For my birthday.

Silence.

And afterwards I got home and I still felt just as shitty as I did before. Worse, actually. And that's when I remembered the book you gave me. It was sitting on my dresser where I'd left it. So I picked up your copy of *Another Country* and I started to read. And almost instantly I felt held again. By you. By Baldwin. How did you know? How did you know I needed that book?

Jonathan I just . . . you asked me to pick out one of my favourites.

Wes Play along a little, can't you?

Jonathan Maybe the books do pick us, after all.

Wes Thank you.

Silence.

Why are you so sad, Jonathan?

This hits Jonathan like a thunderbolt.

Jonathan What makes you think I'm sad?

Wes just looks at him.

Wes Look, I know the whole reason we met was for sex. I'm not naive. Not about that, at least. But, I don't know. Am I wrong? I felt there was a kind of connection between us. I know it's not that much to go on. But I thought that maybe we could – I don't know – maybe we could be friends. Or maybe more than friends. I wouldn't mind that. I'd love that. But at least friends. I mean, I don't know, is that so strange a thing to ask someone?

You don't have to tell me everything at once. Just tell me a little bit. And then a little bit more. And you could just keep telling me until eventually I'd know you. And then maybe I can tell you a little bit about myself and eventually you'd know me, too. And then maybe we'd both feel just a little less alone in the world.

It's just that . . . I think you might be amazing. I think you might be really amazing. And I think that I might be amazing, too. I just don't know.

You push and you push and you push. And then, suddenly, you pull. And that one pull is stronger than all of your pushes combined. That pull makes me wonder what else is there. It makes me want to know more. And the only thing that keeps me from feeling entirely like a fool right now is somehow I have the feeling that maybe you want that, too. Maybe not from me, but from someone. And I'm the one here offering it to you now. So maybe you can let me.

Tell me I'm wrong.
Tell me you're not who I think you are.
Tell me I'm just the most foolish boy in the world.
I promise you: I'll listen.

Wes waits an eternity for Jonathan to respond. But Jonathan doesn't. Wes is anguished at this apparent rejection. He moves to leave. As he does, Jonathan reaches out and grabs him gently by the hand. Then, slowly, Jonathan pulls Wes to him. He intertwines his fingers with Wes's and pulls him into a deep kiss. Wes melts. Finally, the floodgates open and Jonathan begins kissing him with abandon. Jonathan moves Wes to the bed and they begin to grapple and paw at each other. It's frantic and feral. It should be desperate and intense and sexy at the same time. Then suddenly, Jonathan starts to cry. It's a total about-face in energy. He buries his face in Wes's chest and cries.

Whoa. Hey. Hey.

Jonathan cries and holds on to Wes.

Hey.
It's okay, it's okay.

Shhh . . .

Wes holds Jonathan as he cries.

I'm sorry.
Whatever it is, I'm so sorry, Jonathan.
I'm sorry that happened to you.

They hold each other. Jonathan's sobs abate. Silence for a while. Jonathan looks at Wes, falling into him deeply. Jonathan gently kisses him. They hold one another.

I was so afraid you were going to kick me out again.

Jonathan I'm sorry.

Wes It's okay.

Jonathan Thank you.

Kiss.

You are so beautiful.

Kiss.

Kind and compassionate and beautiful, beautiful Wes.

Kiss.

Stay with me. Stay the night.

Kiss.

Wes Okay.

Kiss.

Jonathan I need you.

Kiss.

Wes Yes, of course.

Kiss.

Jonathan I love you.

Wes's heart fills with love.

Wes I love you, too.

They kiss. They laugh. They kiss again. They hold each other.

I made you a playlist.

Jonathan You did not.

Wes I did!

Wes goes to his coat and retrieves his iPhone.

I like to make Spotify playlists in response to different things I encounter in the world. I made one based on *Another Country*.

Wes plugs in his phone and a song starts to play.
Wes starts to sway to the music. Jonathan watches. For a moment, Wes doesn't realise he's being watched. Then he does.

What?

Jonathan I think I may have underestimated you.

Wes I think I may have let you.

They stare at one another. Then Wes returns to the playlist, clicking forward. We hear snippets of the beginnings of songs.

Anyway, I spent hours working on it. I've been listening to it all autumn long. It's just, I don't know, basically the soundtrack for the book. Coltrane and Miles Davis, which I hadn't really listened to. Lots of great jazz drummers and some jazz singers, too. I just kept following the trail and it led to some amazing things. This book opened up a whole new world for me, musically. So thank you for that, too.

Jonathan Come here.

Wes Right. ADHD, I'm sorry. I just want to find the perfect . . . here –

Wes finally lands on a song that he decides to leave on. A Johnny Hartman song starts to play. Jonathan is hit full force by this, as if he has just seen a ghost. Wes returns to Jonathan, quickly taking off his clothes as he does.

Do you know who this is? Oh my God I love him. His name is Johnny Hartman. I'd never heard of him before. He's not mentioned in the book but it's like they must have listened to him.

Wes approaches and starts to kiss him, unbuttoning Jonathan's shirt. Throughout the following, Jonathan slowly starts to implode. He sits down on the sofa.

Jonathan Wes . . .

Wes goes over to Jonathan and straddles him.

Wes.

Wes reaches for Jonathan's jeans and starts to undo them. Jonathan grabs Wes's hand to stop him.

Wes, listen. I don't think I –

Wes It's okay. I know you didn't mean it. But I feel it too.

Wes presses his body into Jonathan's, kissing his face and neck.

Jonathan Wes.
Wes.

Wes Shh . . .
Shh . . .

Wes continues down this path until Jonathan bolts and moves away from him, making a beeline for the stereo and yanking Wes's phone from the jack.

Jonathan?

Jonathan I need you to go.

Wes Go?

Jonathan Please. / I need you to leave.

Wes But Jonathan . . . I don't understand.

Jonathan grabs Wes's things: his clothes, his coat, his iPhone, etc.

Jonathan I don't want you here.

Wes Did I do something wrong?

Jonathan Please get dressed.

Jonathan shoves Wes's stuff at him. Wes lets them fall to the ground.

Wes Please tell me what I did wrong.

Jonathan I just need you to leave.

Wes But why?

Jonathan (*with force*) Just take your shit and go.

Silence a second.

Wes Jonathan? What just happened?

Wes reaches for Jonathan but he bats his hand away.

Jonathan Go.

Wes Please.

Jonathan I don't want you here.

Wes You don't mean that.

Jonathan I do.

Wes Jonathan . . .

Jonathan starts shoving him towards the door like a schoolyard bully.

Jonathan Get out.

Wes Why are you / doing this?

Jonathan Go!

Wes Jonathan, please tell me what I did wrong.

Jonathan grabs Wes tightly by the shoulders.

Jonathan I want you to leave. I need you to / leave.

Wes Jonathan, please don't do this.

Jonathan starts manoeuvring Wes to the door, still holding his arm tightly.

Ow, Jonathan you're hurting me.

Jonathan Get out.

Wes Jonathan, please.

Jonathan shoves Wes into the hallway. Wes falls to the ground. Jonathan then grabs Wes's stuff and hurls it at him.

Jonathan?

Jonathan Leave me alone!

Jonathan slams the door in Wes's face.
  At this, Claire sits up in bed.
  Jonathan gets up, grabs a glass and pours himself an enormous glass of whisky. He gulps it down then pours another. He sits down, burying his face in his hands.
  Claire makes her way to her apartment door, listening.
  Wes – still half naked, bewildered and humiliated – gets to his feet. He wants to knock on the door but is afraid to. He wants to say something but he can't. He starts to cry. He tries not to make any sounds but stifling his cries only seems to make them stronger, less controllable.
  Claire opens her door, steps out onto the landing.

Claire Jonathan?

Wes panics at the sound of her voice. He begins to gather up his things – dressing as quickly as he can – completely disintegrating as he does. By the time he is dressed and has his possessions in hand, he has broken down completely. He lets out a wail of despair and humiliation, then flees out the building.

Claire comes down the stairs just in time to catch Wes as he exits.

A moment, then . . .

Jonathan?

Jonathan, are you okay? Who was that?

Jonathan seizes up at the sound of her voice. He quickly moves to lock the door. He sits down on the floor by the door. She tries to open it.

Jonathan, unlock the door.

Jonathan I can't . . .

Claire Of course you can.

Jonathan I don't know what to do any more.

Claire Please let me in, Jonathan.

He begins to break down. This happens a while: Jonathan on the floor, Claire sitting on the other side.

Jonathan I don't know what I'm supposed to do any more. What am I supposed to do?

Claire It's okay.

Jonathan I have nothing. I have nothing. I have nothing. I have nothing. I have nothing.

Claire That's not true, Jonathan. Please open the door.

Jonathan What am I supposed to do?

Claire Let's go to the Cotswolds. Right now. Let's just go. What do you say, Jonathan? Let's go to the Cotswolds and never come back. Wouldn't that be nice? Let's just pack up and leave and never look back. I can show you how, Jonathan. It's easy. Let's do that, Jonathan, right now. We'll be so happy, I know it. I promise, Jonathan: we don't ever have to be afraid again. Just come with me, please. Let's go.

Jonathan stands, downs the drink and moves to the bedroom. Hearing him moving inside, Claire stands.

Jonathan? Talk to me, Jonathan, please. Don't leave me alone out here. Open the door. Jonathan, please.

Jonathan flops down onto the bed and passes out cold.

6 DEEP, DARK NIGHT

Jonathan stirs awake. He sits up and the events of last night come flooding back to him. We watch him remember it all. He then looks up and calls out:

Jonathan Claire?

He opens his front door and goes into the hallway, looking up at Claire's door.

Claire?

He looks at the stairs as if they will swallow him if he attempts to climb them. He slowly makes his way up to Claire's floor.

Claire? You there?

He climbs the stairs. It is difficult for him. He gets to the door and stands in front of it.

Claire?

He knocks. Nothing. He waits. Then knocks again. And again.

Claire?

His trembling hand reaches for the doorknob. His heart is racing. He turns the knob. It is unlocked. He slowly opens the door and walks inside, terrified. The apartment is pitch black but he does not dare turn on the light.

Claire?

He fumbles for the wall switch. He turns on the light. The apartment is empty. Claire is gone. The camping chair, her clothes, all gone. All that remains is Gabe's painting on the bedroom wall and a trash bag and a broom up by the kitchen.

Claire?

Jonathan looks around the room.

Gabriel?

Through the windows, the room starts to fill with a bright brilliant light.